TO SQUARE A CIRCLE

Poems by

T.K. Lee

Published by Unsolicited Press
www.unsolicitedpress.com

Cover Art by Danielle Bruce
Editor: S.R. Stewart

For information, contact the publisher at
info@unsolicitedpress.com

Unsolicited Press Books are distributed to the trade by Ingram.
Printed in the United States of America.
ISBN: 978-1-947021-53-2

ACKNOWLEDGMENTS

Amanda Clay Powers. Her guidance, her skillful eye, and her patience helped me shape this collection into a story, my first told through poetry. Further, she helped guide me down the rabbit holes, per se, that were necessary to fall into in order to put on the page what needed to be put on the page.

Summer, Rosie, and Unsolicited Press, for the leap they took with me and this collection. Their faith in this work renewed mine in myself.

My family. That hodgepodge of good people who are as dogmatic as they are loving; as difficult and sensible as they are forgiving, who never hesitated in encouraging me to chase after my own star, even though, as a child especially, there were times when it seemed I was looking for that star in unfamiliar skies.

And, lastly, to those whose ears I have bent on many a long evening (or, road trip) reading poem after poem aloud seeking what felt like endless feedback from endless drafts because that's exactly what it was (that's a nod to you, Danielle and Pattye) —thank you for letting your ears bend, then and for the foreseeable future?, and thank you for sometimes just telling me you liked it.

In this collection, several poems have appeared first elsewhere, in various forms. I am grateful for these journals for giving them a chance to be read by the wider public: *The Alembic* ("frogism," "In the Round," and "Cleanliness"); *Serving House* ("Mimic"); *Studio One*

("Pathology"); *The Binnacle* ("Blue Ribbon Woman"); *The Carolina Quarterly* ("Riesling d'Etre"; "Of Monsters"), and *The Furious Gazelle* ("Spelling").

Contents

*to Uncle Larry who was good
when I was good, and better
when I wasn't*

TO SQUARE A CIRCLE

FROGISM

we were fat
never full
& eleven
& cartoons
& jelly
& biscuits
& sugar
& molasses
& butter
& sweet tea
& Coke
& Saturdays
& rain
& the frogs
would pop

up
& sit
on top

of the rocks
& we would
in a sugar high
drag the shovels
from the

mower shed
& sneak

up
on the frogs
& beat
them flat
& thin
until the
metal had
gone through
the frogs
& was only
hitting rock
& it'd be that
certain racket
that drove
Momma mad
but she'd say
oh boys
are being boys
& that
Christmas is
when Daddy
bought us guns,

ESAU IN ITTA BENA, MISSISSIPPI

Michael shot me
by the runner beans,
the smoke—I swear—
coming off
his finger, a solid minute
after I fell
writhing like cotton
mouths, hoe to the head.
I slid
on a clod,
skinned my knee.

Uncle Moon hollering
        "You messing up
          my clean rows,"
in that gumbo dirt
turned over
for the sweet corn
and runner beans
and yellow squash
and red potatoes
was our sandbox
where we playground.

I was still dying when
      Michael said, "Play dead already."
I ground into a fresh pile
of buckshot soil.
Uncle Moon facing
off toward the house.
The sweat in my eyes
hurt. The history of that
Delta sun, how it razed us—
now and there and then—
(I was supposed to be dead)
I was distracted when

Michael said,
(and I'll say it scared me
how his voice had gone low,
sudden
as a separate cloud
an open eye, furrowed)
"You sure play dead like you mean it,"
Michael said,
(And I'll say it. His voice
was already old, deep
      as a set bone).

He set his arm swinging,

that same clod
in his hand,
a stare raked across
his brow
that
(would soon grow
wide
       up to be a Field
       wilder)
filled his cheeks
with an acre of headlong age.

He stood, one leg a posthole
sewn into the ground, a natural fit to
the left leg, bent like a disc
in a tiller. That bend, that's what
did it, yielded him a single mule
of a thought that he mistook
as his birthright:
         He would not be a hand-
me-down nephew with no neck
afraid to look up,
not now that he realized he
had always been an arm-
length away from the sun.

Michael believed that.

Michael believed it
with that full
unbroken circle
of faith that only
favors the young;
                    he thought,
in that moment,
with enough, with his own, momentum,
        he could throw
that same clod
(picked up from a plow-perfect row of loam)
straight to the sun,
past the cloud, alone
past the clouds, all together

the World, in one throw
at the end of his fist

Here he was
A would-be king of dirt, born
(before long—boring)
holes in the roots around his ankle,
gathering stray pine limbs or
Bradford Pear switch-sticks to tether
his dingy white socks to
surrender
To Do Again What's Been Done

For the Last Hundred Years:
          Stay Here and Still

Michael,
tall as he is
he is
a self-fulfilled scarecrow
prophecy. You can see
him from the road
far and away
high above
          the runner beans,
          the yellow squash,
          the red potatoes,
          the sweet corn.

 He, would-be king,

      of eventual rot
sick to death
but not
dying. This is the lesson
I learned
face down in the dirt,
where he left me
for dead.

THE BLAME AND THE BREATH

MaOnie's thin
watch kept ticking, I saw
seconds spin little loose wheels
in the rut of her wrist.
The rest of her
visible body, so waned, it
looked gone,
looked lived in

that powder
blue blouse beneath
that powder
blue blazer
and her shawl.
And her makeup
meant to make her familiar,
make her still,
matter,
to me. This was my first death.

It was easier than
my second
death came soon after.

This is what it looked like:
       A voluntary, manmade breath
       in the same clothes. You didn't change

from the funeral...
       This was your weekend.

       Gas was no guarantee
to the mother you gave me.
She wouldn't let you
see me, say
on a Monday,
       if she was out of coffee and kept forgetting to get
       coffee.
On a Thursday,
       if she found a headache in the closet or the
       backseat.
Often, this shock of interruptions
lasted the entire week before you

       your used Datsun
and   her used Toronado
and   my used Sears Spyder
       What a moment, airy postcard
       we made
       of that unused carport.

She let you
love me
        if you kept the receipts.

I was quite the child.
Quite with
quiet

resolve you stood out where the iris come in April.
I watched you from the kitchen
my hand
in the hand
of the other woman
        as you ruined
        your Duckheads and a button-up
        for a small hole
                at the mercy of the neighbor's shovel
                        as you bent down
        for the Florsheim shoe box, looking—how quick—
        like a life gone off on its own

[except this is not a nursery rhyme]

        like a life.

                Gone.
                Off.

An accident
with the cat: It was the cat's fault.
                 It was your fault.
                 It was nobody's fault. That's what an accident
means.
I kept my seatbelt on. We talked for several long
minutes before I cried.

"Cars are big. Cats are not." and
"Four tires versus four legs" and
"Machine against Man.
        Well,
        Animal."

The other woman had by this point
crawled outside
the car staring
at everything else
        the tear in the Welcome Mat, I bet
        the moldy garden hose, I bet
        the back of my uncle's unpainted house, I bet.

"Family!" I said and I didn't say it quietly.

"You can get another cat."
"You can get another car!"

I started
        to lie just now

to say I heard you but
the truth is
        what you said to yourself
        that day out in the yard was
                probably baby words about grown up regret,
                probably average words about absent
fathers,
                probably. I could see you,
        each labored breath.
        You were on fire, I saw the smoke.
I witnessed you,
back into your shoulders, into the rain,
into the needle-cold, a vigilante of faith.

        Even the throaty nut-grass gave way,
        as you pulled the very Earth from itself,
        a shovel at a time.

When it was done: the digging, the burying,
the blame smoked from a whole pack of breath,
the look on your face—like a 12-gauge had
been shot too few yards from the house—
that look
        tore into the glass,

tore through the curtains,
  tore up the carpet, and after, that
          look sat there
in a den too big for a den
of such size demanding worship
of your sweat

    because nothing is more honest than sweat

(The way of fathers, they say, and it is
the way of children, they say, usually
yes) but—

what I've come to understand:
There once lived a father who could plant death.
There once lived a father who could...
There once lived a father
there, once.

OF MONSTERS

A monster is easily born
if you know the right nursery rhyme.
Go on, lock your door. Blow your horn
time after time after time

if you know the right nursery rhyme
you'll understand the Moon is
(time after time after time)
simply playing the Fool. Soon

you'll understand the Moon is
no better than the Wolf for
simply playing the Fool. Soon
enough, every one of us keeps score,

no better than the Wolf for—
never mind. Children will learn
 enough. Every one of us keeps score
turn after turn after turn,

never mind. Children will learn
a monster is easily born
turn after turn after turn.

24

Go on, lock your door. Blow your horn.

RUT

a carousel   spins—
a dragon chases
a fox with wings,
following a chariot
pulled eyeless by
a giant owl; a boy
clasps   a metal pole—
the back   of a white stag—
goes round once,
once is twice; he
becomes a man
aware that a crowd
now gathers around,
the circle, murmuring,
the crowd,   they stare—
less   at the boy; more—
at the idea of a fair
people, all those in
the crowd that he has
become, they stare
too, each time he
passes by: the lion,
with its rotten mouth

open: a lion, riderless
always   at his heels—

ANOTHER BIRTHDAY

And so, he had his piece of cake. After he cried,
his mother said, "Hush, now, and open this." Beside
him, his sister, his spit on her face, wads of snot.
Mixed paper plates and forks, melting ice cream, and not
one nice thing even said about the boy. She lied

again, "Your father will be here soon." How she tried:
He had slapped her earlier at church. On the ride
home he said dirty words. But the cake had been bought
and so, he had his piece of cake after he cried.

Open that: penknife. Open this: BBs. With hide
and seek to come. Pictures of the kids side by side.
She's angry: All she has loved is all she has fought
for. But, this was her house and though there wasn't a lot
he was still her son, "Here," she says, "Open up wide."
And so, he had his piece of cake. After, he cried.

FIT

...my uncle (not my mother) folds the fitted sheets,
makes all the beds even. I am ten, at least,
when my uncle (not my mother) takes an afternoon
to show me: How to crisp the corners, iron the crease.
(He was born a bachelor, she used to make-believe).
Then, I am twenty, and then, I am thirty, and soon—
old enough to have a similar house on a similar street
in a similar (uncompromising) bed I keep very clean:
Hobnail, softest iron; mattress, firm as a virgin's broom.
Best laid plans still have to be laid—or is it led?
(Here's to the legacy of the well-made bed).

BLUE RIBBON WOMAN

Her focus on the dough lying
boneless on the counter
is disturbing. Her hands,
maniacal and powdered
from wheat's blood,
the scent of yeast

on her knuckles, she arches
her back; she surgically removes
bread from common ingredients
in the cabinet. She speaks

in handfuls—
    finger-dashes of how—she doesn't believe
I've been orphaned
by the kitchen.

She closes the lid on an age-
less Tupperware bowl.
She pushes it, arbitrarily,
toward the sink
to wait for a natural magic.

She returns to the present; now,
she makes a Monday dinner
for a Monday family. I can't stand
long while it's still her kitchen—
I'd be in her way—watching
her back do
the simplest of tasks
with the arthritis of her pioneers.

What's good and right will
    always rise. At least, she has

her pride, her rural language. Upset
that strength has left her with home-
made hands, she's still fed me

for years on the lie
of good cornbread to keep me
facedown in a full plate;

    she has never seen me,
never talked to me, simply
asked that I set
the table. So, I set
the table

    while she won

three ribbons for her sweet
potato pie,
two for her pepper
jelly.

TO SQUARE A CIRCLE

/

When I crawled
into the red-clay hills behind
Uncle Moon's house,
I climbed and fell,

on purpose, but you couldn't
tell it from the road like you could
the things that some boys did.

Choctaw pop rocks broke under
the weight of history in my belly
force fed by fistfuls,
they spilled
open, they spread burnt
oranges, rust irons, pale ochers,
each a dirty pig-
ment, native
to the gulley floor.

There was a grandmother then
with kept fingers
on her brow

looking eager for land in my eyes
off the back porch,
summer on the back of summer
gone wild in my ankle.
I made her eyes hurt.

Elbows and knees and chin and shoulders
stitched in dirt.
                          I smelled only of the outside;
  a perfume she hadn't worn on the neck
  for a thousand years.

//
Her son grew up to be an uncle
  who never took his mouth off the sugar tit.
Her daughter grew up to belong
   to there and then and that and this

Time came,
a gentleman at the door.
The grandmother died and left
the house to her son;
the world to her daughter,

but not before she learned—
      though it sounded like a yell—

a song written for the kitchen
meant for scrambled eggs
or tomato sandwiches
or meatloaf.

Against the grit in the grandson,
it tore into a homily
with tall, new words
      that came out already bent
into a shape she was accustomed to—
a garden variety church hymn
   that she could hum one end
of the house to the next,
that she could use ,
as a blessing over the food
      on the table—
which made her repeat herself.
Which made her stop humming.
Which left her then only able to
say, "Be quiet.
      Clean your plate."

Which he did, each single time.

///
The way he ate
when he ate,

scared her.

SPELLING

A once-and-again mother picks at her teeth
at the Sunday dinner table, laughing at how
her church must be the only church
where there was no need for a gun.

She takes the fat off the roast, drags a piece
through carrots, coleslaw, across her plate.
"We're Christian people," she said, "All
of us good. We don't need no guns. Yet."

She has her a J.R. pistol: Colt, black, white-
handled, an uncle's gift, years ago
in a bedside table drawer for safekeeping
under a pair of folded gloves, loaded.

(Nobody wears gloves anymore).
Instead: "Every seat's a backseat these days,"
she changes the subject. (It's her hobby)
She changes subjects (she keeps the change).

She dips a chintzy sleeve in the pear salad
on her way to a fourth helping of the potatoes.
(She pretends not to notice the dirty sleeve

so she doesn't have to notice the pear salad).

An only son sits across from her,
(There are six chairs that go with this table),
his plate cleaned beneath him. All by himself,
he skillfully develops an afternoon headache

watching her watching her dirty her sleeve.
(It matters to her that the gun is mostly black.
She's mentioned it two times now and he's—
"I'm gonna wear those gloves I don't care where!"

She never uses her napkin. She should.
"I'll wear them to Piggly Wiggly for bananas!"—
Small bits of corn have breaded her blouse.
It's a lovely Sunday to be embarrassed), he nods,

to himself. She nods for a different reason.
He re-positions himself on the piano bench.
(He's never had a chair at this table)
by the sliding glass door – Breaking

news— the TV is on—Mississippi has the worst
economy in the nation—the TV stays on—
"Cheap bananas," she says, "Even the new ones."
There's nothing new in Mississippi anymore.

(There's nothing in Mississippi anymore).
Mississippi's not even in Mississippi anymore.
This is it – the bang. Come out, come out.
Hide and Seek, not Red Rover, Red Rover.

He considers having more roast beef.
The end of the world, if it's coming, come
put your deer in the road already, come
cut out Piggly -Wiggly-bag-magnolias,

press those steeple-fingers up against
the knotted threads of catfish wool;
throw rice at the cows lowing their famous
bathrobe song in that Bethlehem key.

"Aunt Lola died. Did I tell you." (No,
forget the roast beef. Maybe pear salad).
A mockingbird then flies headfirst in
to the sliding glass doors. She had

a finger in her mouth; she bit it, but
she didn't turn. She won't look out at
the pecan trees, left after Katrina, still
stubbed, like dotted, crooked letters,

waiting for one last word. Some say
it'll be a hand-me-down tablecloth;

or, the tragedy of a hobnail milk glass
vase broken into favors. Or, smaller like

the deep freeze or the goddamn world.
The end: The Big Bang's Ready or Not.
No more hiding places left in the napkins.
Nothing familiar is left on the forks.

"The chandelier would be pretty
if it weren't so dusty. I don't know
how on earth to go about cleaning
a chandelier. And one that old."

She says this easy. How she moves
from the gun to gloves to bananas
from Aunt Lola to the old chandelier,
happens quickly, happens every Sunday,

reliable as a boil water notice. She's a boil
water notice. Newsworthy. Reliable, yes.
Except you're not sure exactly whose faucet.
She could be someone else's faucet,

next door or the next door. Or the next.
He looks up. The table is empty now.
He carries the bench and puts it back
in front of the upright and the living

room's back the same; he has the same
thought, back, behind his headache:
The fact of a bench is that it isn't a chair.
The fact is, it does not need a table.

RIESLING D'ETRE

The feel of a napkin has lost its sentiment
over the years. But then, so has the concept
of a forest, and in her hands, fingers bent
was a glass of the house Riesling, the stem wet
from a near accident: a spill when the glass almost fell.
It only slid, much as we had, shoulder into shoulder
and conversations were too fragile, I could tell
she was trying to listen, but other
than a small tilt of her head, she had half her
lipstick leaving its smile around the rim
of Riesling, cooling itself into lukewarm and laughter.
She simply wasn't interested in him.
He didn't notice, and took out his ballpoint pen,
grabbed a napkin and wrote his number down,
he did his mating dance: to leave and then leave again.
The imprint on her glass began to frown.
There's no sentiment in such frivolous men, either;
She knows they tear the forests up for themselves.
She sighed asking for another glass, but sweeter;
then, started counting all the glasses she had left.

MIMIC

Tony Bennett is in my bathroom. He is
singing, in the bathroom, wide awake, while
the house stands, singular, constant, as it sits
beneath the usual weight of a drunk loose Noun.
The dog's asleep. No, he died in June, that's right.
The cat is asleep. I went sightseeing in the kitchen,
a loudmouth tourist in cabinets, lost and found first
by the stove; second, by the last good back door
in America that I know of. It's a shame that
I haven't replaced those blinds. It's no way
to treat a good back door's window-wife. If
it weren't for the rust-frown of the chain-link fence
a carousel of strangers could come up the back steps—
peek-a-boo!—catalogue my eating habits: crackers /
mayonnaise / gin / boiled eggs / tuna / gin /
Kraft singles / coffee coffee coffee / gin gin gin
begins again this afternoon with ~~warm~~, sorry, worn
pajama legs for napkins; Ziploc leftovers, left over.
Yes, Tony Bennett is in my bathroom, that's where
I keep the CD player. I still listen to CDs. I still
make the hairbrush a microphone. I still sing along.
I know these words by blackout. "Your looks are /
laughable / un-photographable / yet you are

my favorite work"—there's an alarm suddenly.
Suddenly the whole goddamn house is a Verb.
I'm late for work again I'm in the bathroom again,
hairbrush in hand. Tony's finished. I can't seem to.
The off-brand light bulb above the mirror, it pops,
goes dark, my only applause. This mirror. I have
thrown up on it. I see vomit in the sink, I have
it in my hair. I brush it out with my microphone—
I sing in the same wet flat key as my mother—
I stand eye-to-eye with a face full of Fool's Gold.
The mirror frame, the backyard fence, one square
reflexive property re-mortgaged for a song.
With the patience of walls, I stand in the frame
until I make myself jealous. I stand in the frame,
singular, constant, usual, wide awake, staring
at the look of another thousand words, wasted.

PATHOLOGY

Some men are born to cry uncle
with their father-hands, their mother-mouths.
Mine has also worn the same thing for years:
a flour-sack apron, a belt of mirrors

tied around his waist with sweet potato vine,
which he tied to my waist as well.
He fingers the vine daily, a rosary he made
himself, a green badge of loneliness.

I learned early on that it takes a tornado to get him
to stand still long enough. To hear me, to see me,
I have even uprooted the trees myself—
a lie in the wind—that grow back in his ears.

It takes the likes of Job to wait for tornadoes.
It's hard work uprooting trees. More than once,
I've planted whispers in the holes they left, hoping
they didn't grow away; they blossomed shade.

I chose my words like any borrowed child
would. They were hoarse and dry
so they might blend into the sound of cattle

grazing, catfish frying, into something familiar.

He would not let me be alone. Like him,
We lived in the kitchen. Among skillets
as wide as hours. Among jars of bacon grease
slowly milking themselves into gospeled halves.

It is his kitchen. It is his house. Here, he's
hung mountains on the walls. What little sun
 snakes through each morning is wound
with sweet potato vine into another knot.

The sun-sliver then sets behind the steeple
across the road of the church he built.
The preacher, who calls him by his name,
comes by for scraps, his hands for plates.

His plain, simple house, it isn't mine. Yes, it has
 stood against tornadoes. Yes, he has fed me
the pain of land, brick, the haul of the crop,
leftovers, so often the spoon rarely left my mouth.

Yes, I choked. Yes, I left him. I left him
while he slept in what looked like ruin. But
I walked away, a timid young man not yet
realizing that his legs could run.

I got as far as the gate when it happened.

He woke. It was the draft from the open
screen door—caught a leg in the mesh. It cried out.
His gardened face dug up from a deep sleep,

he leaned against one of his mountains, staring,
while he grabbed the vine and gave it a pull.
I went back up the knotted, gravel drive,
my face clearly visible in his apron.

PIECEMEAL

I: An Everyman For All Seasons

That, let's say, first time: Before we gave up
before the closest, youngest kid at hand was forced
into *God is Great and Amen*,
we sat down and talked like people do
about what people talk about:
the weather and the dead and food.

It didn't have to be at a kitchen table.
(Some of us never had a kitchen table.
Some of us lost our kitchen tables,
one August,
one April.
'A porch swing will do fine',
was how the joke started. Still,
it was better with a plate, we kept on saying for some
reason
plates do better on kitchen tables far
from the danger of an open lap—
         if the plate spills, or
         if you're in your church pants, or
         if it's MaOnie's meatloaf, or

48

if the plate spills and
       you're in your church pants and

       it's MaOnie's meatloaf
       and you forgot to say Amen.
       You forgot—you shouldn't eat on porch swings.

You were so good at starting
that you never bothered to finish.
One time (it was more than one time)
you left your plate on that porch swing.
It looked like a piece of meatloaf
was trying to crawl away.
It was
sugar ants. They
took their time,
and ate and ate and ate
and took the rest of that
good meatloaf right off your plate
so neatly pinched that really
there wasn't much left
to talk about after awhile

II. Snakes, Snails, and the Like

There was that other time:

one of Miss/Ms./Mrs. Wilma's guineas—
promise you won't forget
how they would sit
up in that magnolia
the live-long day,
        a plump orchestra
of live-long racket—
                got hit by a car.

The sound, a fist to mud.

The feathers flew further than the bird
ever had. Or did.
We were two kids,
who had missed the school bus
who had a typical Monday morning.

    She was
     a girl from the high school,

the one who needed the bra
(and one of us knew better
than to say the word *bra*
and one of us knew better
because of the bra)
with the thick straps, didn't she
        show you those straps,

on the hayride we went on
that we were too young for,

in her mother's Monte Carlo

part-Choctaw.
She didn't stop.

The T-Tops gone with Boy George
coming out loud
as a single feather
 in
perched on the forehead
of the driver's side visor.

It was your first Indian Summer, that October.
It was your first—what did we decide to call it,
"Big Bone Moment"?
          A couple of dumb boys, us. Fine:
It was Your Big Bone Moment—
   you turned to me, said That Girl
was Magic stacked in denim,
a perfume spell
under all that hay.

You too were Wunderkind,
a real-live abracadabra.

The Wayward and The Wand-less.

You figured it out
the secret, you found
that the long-in-the-tooth luck
of feathers,
      guinea or otherwise,
      (so rarely within arm's reach)
belongs to those who won't
hesitate when the Commonplace
becomes the Extraordinary
  when a Monte Carlo schools you
  with nothing but the break/blow/burn[1]
  of a clutch. Your head turned
  following her down the road

   (and then one of us was left)
with the wonder
of it,
of how
very much fits
onto the rib of a single feather,
of how
heavy such light
things can weigh.

-----

[1] John Donne's "Batter my heart, three-person'd God"

I like to say now: I hate the feather
took wing to the very car
that only set it free
by killing everything
else around it.

III. A Poetry Handbook

That Easter—were we even
                    old enough to be kids yet?—
on account of the rain which was sent down
with a smell: The used flint of cheap matches—
the world's longest conversation began
between us.

    No.

(One of us hadn't been born yet. Wait.

    No.

Neither of us had been born yet).

    This is the clipped wick of history
having hooked its knuckle on the spider web

above the washing machine

that works and doesn't work
that we all won't quit talking about
how it works but doesn't work. Instead,
we look out whatever window is closest
we say,

"We should talk about something else. The flood
was years and years ago," except we don't.
We say,

"We should get a new washing machine.
We should sweep away those spider webs,"
except we don't.

We don't
talk about anything else except how we wish we would talk
about anything else.

The Old Uncle Man says, "Oh the yard."
The yard used to be a pond,
        how the pond had bream,
        how the yard has calla lilies,
        how the yard used to be
    a pond that used to have bream
        but now has calla lilies
"It's too much rain,"

the Old Uncle Man says, "We needed the rain."
Old Men,
after they go mad at night[2], never see again
that the way they approach the kitchen sink,
for instance, or the crockpot,
eats them up,
bites them with Time.

Don't we
all look the same in the dark[3]?, you think
being eaten
like this needs
a brief explanation:
  This Hour at dawn is
  That Hour at dusk is
  The Same Hour and
  they have each
collapsed, These Hours,
  into a dark boast
of soot-ash all through
the house   that cloying
gray coats the hearth
which needs cleaning
every day,

---

[2] Cf: Tennessee Williams' poem, "Old Men Go Mad At Night"
[3] Cf: Shel Silverstein's poem, "No Difference"

every day, he needs it to

need cleaning. Everyday).

These Old Men,
armed with small liver spots
ad infinitum, ad nauseum,
e pluribus unum, this Old Uncle Man
made going mad a day-
time hobby fossilizing lunch
for dinner slowed and shrunk
to the size of the
last will and testament
of a dent in
an Overall button.
Old Men lose
their sight, usually,
in that cold, front
part of the Living Room that they don't use
after good children die,
       according to custom.

It's in this room, I'd guess
beside the upright piano
beneath the cracking corner mold
with a few thickened family portraits
tin-typed into the flock-

                    ed wallpaper,
          so peeled
from years of being looked at,

from years of standing up straight,
          it seems constantly caught
escaping half-winged
          in mid-flight.

It's in this room, where Old Men might,
if it's not too hot,
if it's not too cold,
remember standing up straight
remember being looked at, too,
   but not why they still come
   into the Living Room
for the sole
purpose of convincing themselves
that cold biscuits with tomato gravy,
matter,

(Mattered—
to one of us).
Maybe

what used to be in line
of sight dissolves into sound

the older we get.
       (One of us anyway). Yet,
the safety in that sentiment
is lost. Almost immediately,

Old Men start chewing
their tongues—
tethers, lip to jaw,
without slack, on the tips,
a prerecorded prayer
memorized in a muscle
of flesh weak with revival

(One of us helped set up
the folding chairs at the church
because we had to but)
let's not think of what can be
caught on a chewed tongue
in the habit of not choosing
a hill to die on
       (You remember, don't you,
how Old Uncle Man went
       on about hills to die on).

       The Old Uncle Man will
perform a last rite
in the Living Room

before walking back into the rest
of the house.

He will say things like:
> That was his toothbrush (he meant you)
> That was his pillow case (he meant you)
> That was his BB gun (he didn't mean me)
> That was his potato peeler (he meant
> that these things aren't in the Living
> Room).

Both of us, we are in his mind, reminding
him of toddlers discounting
cradle to borrowed playpen.
A blank check,
a handful of Sorry,
a Knuckle's worth
of an old
man's worry dropped on
the floor the same size
of the corners
in
every room of the house—
each corner is its own
 knuckle
under-
foot).

          Steps
into the den,
he forgets that:

Living—

                    Rooms—I can't explain
                    why they run together while
they look the same, house to house. I suppose
it's a small kindness for Old Men
that kids say what they see,

but our Old Uncle Man's Eye
couldn't make a whole circle.
That's why
one of us laid claim to his Old
Ear which made one of us
cruel, didn't it?, because that left
     only one
          of   us
               here

                              in this Old
                              Man's house

                    where the young catch on
                    that the young don't hold on

when the young think that

reminds me
how I was once

the Christ-candy,
legs of spice, a pepper,
meant to offer this
insight

from a toothbrush or a potato peeler
to Even, Old Men:

Let a room alone
so it can do
what it wants to:

disappear.

IV. Odd and Invented Forms

Then, there was that other time, that one
of us fell asleep
and woke up. It was the whole next day
and the sun was still in the same place
and the same fever was on the forehead.

61

It wasn't funny then either. We had to
almost grow up and wasn't that something.

We were going to write a a song
to sing. You never could
make your mind up: Sad songs don't sound the same kind
of sad on every
ear...
(Besides: We were too young then to know
what rhymed with pencil.
We were too young then to know
what a song even was).

Remember that night we went to bed and we both
had the exact same dream? I can't remember it clearly.
There was a tire swing, there was a small creek,
there were Pentecostal women
in denim skirts, ankle-deep,
when
we woke up. We didn't much care
for jokes, after that.
We had already turned
thirteen.

There was a glass of water you rolled over into,
knocked it off the bedside table.
A table really ought to learn to keep to itself,

to be more like a porch swing,
      or a porch,
      or a swing,
      (One of us thought the sun
hadn't moved. One of us thought
the sun had stayed
      in the same place,
             that fever made us silly):
         "Go eat
a feather off that guinea
out in the yard, for godsake,"
is what I said.

        (I think you did laugh at that,
              actually).

V. A Bit of Shell

The guinea split quite fairly
in two pieces, after the car;
one piece was not necessarily larger
than the other piece.

The neck, the beak, a leg—you have
to remember this, fell
      into the preacher's yard—well

into that scraggle bridal bush—
and that leg hung itself,
took a limb of its own,
desperately trying to look
like a leaf
  (Let's suppose that dead things still long for
  purpose)

The second leg, the breast, yes,

but the belly
(we shouldn't have laughed so hard)
it landed, upright, took a seat in the ditch
round and fat
like a divorced father,
returning home,
desperate
for a normal cup of coffee.
(Let's suppose there are many
      ways to misspell "desperate").

A few feet from over
beside our stubborn-wonderful
Terabithian metal culvert

            lay an egg
            not quite ready

                    to be an egg

It was an impeccable oval,
                        opaque,
                        hush-pink in color

It was

            an egg

of jelly
you shook it with the heel of your new Sperrys
                    (one of us vomited on the egg,
                    a perfect serving of aspic,
at the way it responded to your shoe.
                    One of us vomited again
in the gravel driveway).

Her name was Candace, you finally said.
She was a sophomore.
She'd said you were cool.
For a seventh grader.

VI. The Two-Hand Follow

Later, and it was much later, wasn't it?,

I noticed you
were only eating tomatoes.

The Old Uncle Man noticed it too.
There's not much threat in a tomato.
He didn't worry until they were tomato_es_
which, in other words, meant
it was too late

                                        then.

We'd put them side by side, the tomatoes,
size to shape and so on, a Chorus Line
across the counter: row-row-row. Your Bowl
for soup washed out to be Your Bowl
for cereal rinsed out to rise up
a Bowl meant for a routine meal of nothing
but cut-up tomatoes.

Gone went the Lehman's candies.
Gone went the sugar biscuit breakfasts.
Gone went the milkshakes at the Chicken Basket.
Gone went the weekend potato chip sandwiches.

        The table, full of chairs, sat empty
                of food/of plates/of seconds/of fuss
                of leftovers/of use
                of us

66

Nothing but tomatoes.
Nothing but a Bowl of tomatoes.
No, a bowl.
A dumb bowl with a lower case "b".

What is that, what is a bowl with a lower case "b"?
Jealous, that's what. You can tell.
Look at any bowl: Round with regret.
Spending its days wanting to break
its back flat like a plate.

There were thirty-one days that June.
July—what is that, what is July—?
                    (We only made it to seven—
one of us caught in a pecan tree
one of us on fire
one of us with a stray bottle rocket)

The feist came back, bald, ears to tail.
Yes, it was the neighbor's dog,
but it was nice to know it came back.

VII. How To Be Beside Yourself

Here's a short list of What You Need
To Know About Living
Everyday
With a Dinosaur,
                         Before
you ask:

These are in a particular order.

- They forget not one goddamn thing.
- They like a closed door. Leave the doors closed if they're closed. Especially when they wander into the Living Room, or stand at the Piano.
- They want the windows open, but not the curtains.
- They keep the TV on. It is best you pretend that you don't know what a TV is.
- They vacuum the iron and iron the vacuum.
- They do not appreciate conversation. Use pictures instead.
- They wedge a knife in the front door, at night, so they can rest. You will cut your food with this knife. You will wash it by hand.
- They go to church, to Piggly Wiggly, and to bed. On Sundays, they do each of these twice. Keep the car gassed up.
- They use the same fork for all meals. Don't wash it. Say nothing when they mistaken the potato peeler for a fork.
- They will never touch another tomato.

VIII. To Live In Meanwhile

Later, and it was much later, it was—
I know this is 100% true.

(One of us died

because
        one of us had to).

CLEANLINESS

/

He never learned
to dance. He learned
to vacuum.

An only child
of an only mother.

He slept on the ironing board;
his work week in the skillet.

He was denied
the privilege of losing
her. Over time
she grew down,
into a wrinkle of quiet,

a wooden sound
familiar as her rocking
chair framed in the sliding glass
doors; he noticed
one ordinary Saturday evening—

　　　　　he was in the process of hanging
　　　　　up a pressed Sunday shirt—
that her rocker
wasn't rocking.

How
　he carried her, a courtesy,
　to the cemetery,
How
　he came home,
　undressed,
How
　he started to vacuum.

I saw this
from behind the couch
from where I'd sneaked in
to watch them
watch TV;

an only grandchild,

I sat and I saw
what I shouldn't though
it's still
my favorite episode
of *Good Times*.

//

Me
a mother left
me, there
I sat so often

to watch him
dancing,
holding the cord—up—
        a skirt's hem,
a curtsy,
to the *Price is Right*.

His gentle hand
guiding,
careful
steps across the floor
bending
tenderly to feel
less impolite
staring,

from the recliner
from the hearth
from the rocking chair
from the couch

from the coffee table

as they waltzed
his sock feet pressing flat
circles in the fresh till
of the unturned carpet

How
      he hummed for his mother
      not mine.
How
      they danced
      down the hall
      in time
      to *All My Children*.

///

I brought my own
once
sat them down
      (the deviled eggs)
along that same couch
him and that vacuum
in that same pas de deux
but barefoot now,

The children laughed—
       he had no toenails—
before we saw
       him stumble—

       his humming stopped.

Those two,
Man and Vacuum,
side-stepped a corner—
       the plug pulled from the outlet—
it was one small misstep—

How
       they fell.

"Sh," I said to the children.

(This is the part where you believe
the swan dies, if it's done well)

Hidden from us
he'd gone

(from the living
             room)

We heard nothing

but applause
for that lucky woman
on the *Wheel of Fortune*.

ARTIFACT

She sits in an arrogant rocking chair
grown into the soft belly of her back
where the cushion ties have worn through.
Her arms bent; scales of fat have bent
them into second elbows. So weighted, she's
a monument, she says, a reminder-stone of
a secret known only to the old: that hidden
in a rocking chair is a grain of immortality.
(Arrogance). She can't stand up on her own.
She offers a hard-boiled hand to the distant
grandson, five whole feet away, he sits done
in by the rust of the Dutch swing, mosquitoes,
by the metaphor of Pine Belt porches.
He hasn't reached out for her. She leaves
her hand there, hanging in the air unsure
if it's hers. *Still, a hand shouldn't linger*.
If it's hers, she'll need it, proof that she is
a woman with her own two hands at least.
(There was no secret in her rocking chair).
Her dead-fish hair is knitted into a bun
under a faded spit-curl wig that has begun
to bob her thoughts along the surface

today. Today she's outstepped—the—
the—the last time she could use her
legs, she had good reason to. She'd been
dancing at her wedding, her father smiling.
She shifts, as if in similar effort now.
The rocking chair took notice. It did
a slight lean in. The distant grandson
took notice. He leaned in, a hand out to
hush her in that preacher-way he stole
from a back pew. Her voice comes out
scattershot to the mailbox, burning, yelling,
"Wash your mouth out with the hose!"
(Lies are how the dying play make-believe).
Then, she forgets the porch, rocking chair.
Her red-moon umbrella of veins appears
as she nods toward understanding that all
that's left is to nod toward understanding.
She is public domain. She is removable fiction:
Hip, teeth, wig, glasses, a breast, oxygen—
she could be taken fully apart, thrown
in the closet to wait the long year out
with the Piggly Wiggly sacks of Christmas
lights, icicles. (Close by. Out of the way).
Her good hand swats at a mosquito.
(Five feet is a dangerous distance).
Her good hand misses the mosquito.
A bite. The itch takes a moment. Yet,

the scratch is violent in an instant, as
sudden as this strange man is beside her
so calmly there among the mosquitoes.
She marvels at that, at how he stands
now against the Dutch swing, at how he
helps her up, steadies her, invites himself
in for supper—*It's supper, he says*—like
the only thing in the world that matters
is to sit down with an old woman, to eat
day-old cornbread with day-old peas.

DUTCH SWING

No, red birds
never sing
in this yard. Once,
above the well, I saw
one fall—
neck rock hard in a baptized noose.
Same rope we all
use to pull
us to church.

IN THE ROUND

The beige recliner by the sliding glass door.
I sit beside you in the rocking chair.
There aren't many words spoken, or
you motion for water, or are you pointing into the air?
I wait for the whimper.

The side table, crowded with bottles of pills.
The oxygen tank as normal as the floor lamp.
I keep the curtains open because the wild turkeys still
come from the woods each morning. Your skin is damp.
I can't hold your whole hand

I can't hold—your whole hand
makes the effort, so I rub your fingers and leave it at that.
There are many things we will leave this way: man
and boy. Father and son. The air in the room is flat.
It makes dying simpler.

Your bangs, strings, have grown frayed.
I brush them out of your face. What matters
now is to lie to you. I spend many hours, a waste,
telling you the azaleas are blooming. The clematis.
The squash, tomato plants.

When/ another long morning is suddenly noon
When/ eyelids flutter—those desperate wings
beat against a mortal jar—When/ lips open to loosen
moans caught on the teeth; When/ fingers, damp things,
gesture for a lament...

Then. No more sponge baths, catheters, cancelled plans.
I melt. I melt there in the living room and make a mess.
The pills won't have to be counted again.
I won't have to clean up the urine, the feces.
I'm the last accident.

I lean back in the rocking chair; a moment after
I brush my bangs back, pull a curl from my hot forehead.
I honestly can't decide if I should cry or laugh or
call an ambulance. I take a deep breath, instead.
Death has a selfish bent.

THE SKIN OF WATER

/
Water seeks its own
level. Imagine
a bare spur, a spine of bank
bread–brown, nervous
as a footnote, branched off an early hand
too soon knuckled to make a river

of a shovelful
of stamped cotton mud
of leaves and leaving.
I don't belong to this water,
but I have seen this water,
up close enough

to know it is better to stand
well beyond the reach of those
who have bluffed their castles; each
man to a levy, a wolf on top a sheep's wall.

This water hides within the river.
a thousand miles of fault.

//
The fat potato caps
of peeled foam
the Gulf throws out its back
door along
the coastline thin into
a lie: The sound to the limp salt

you hear of this
sidewalk-water is hooked
to the old hat of a highway brimmed by ditches
manmaking
a beach out of that lie, bragging of bought sand,
bored as it was into flat local shapes
of boats poked awake—

      as if by effort they can save
      the water from its wet,
imagine that.
The back door gathers,
water on the step,

a knowing brown—the whole round rim
circling this bowl of coast is.
Too soon,
what the boat finds waiting at

the front door is the back door,
the step full of the same
different bags of potatoes,
the few left to peel, soaked
through with a wet
cunning and unsound.

I've seen that water, as well.
It doesn't belong to me, either.

///
I come from plain dish water
like my mother before me
with a rag-draped love that stayed
to prune the kitchen sink—we drank

what we didn't use for dishes—that hung
over the faucet, face down
to the drain. In the dark, we pretended that

even plain dish water remembers
how it came to belong to sinks
how it once carved mountains
how it is still a thing to fear,
like the gulf or the levy or the river.

It is the dish water

       that is here
       preparing
the coming flood—
       a strike of lightning, a stroke of luck,
       that left two black dots
       of spigot-teeth on the water heater.

When we woke up
the den
the kitchen
the carport
had disappeared.

There was water outside wanting in;
rain in rain in rain.
But: Here was water inside,
loose, conscious,
swallowing whole, the house
having collected every thing
but itself.

And: There, outside,
       that water mocked,
up against the sliding glass doors,
       the plain dish water.
Neck and neck, at each other,
one water to another

running
seeking
nothing but the ground

below the den
is the same ground
of rivers of levies of gulfs
of oceans, even,
of even mountains
        of even kitchen sinks.

        Imagine that.
All water runs out of anger
        against the lie
that it is only
meant for the ground when it knows
that it came
        from the sky.

ABOUT THE AUTHOR

 T.K. LEE is an award-winning member of the Dramatists Guild of America and the Society for Stage Directors and Choreographers, among others. A writer of both award-winning short fiction and poetry, he teaches playwriting in the MFA program at the Mississippi University for Women, in Columbus, Mississippi.

For more information, you may visit his website at www.tkleewriting.com or follow him on Facebook.

ABOUT THE PRESS

UNSOLICITED PRESS is a small press in Portland, Oregon. Founded in 2012, the press seeks to produce exemplary poetry, fiction, and creative nonfiction. Authors include Francis Daulerio, David Wasserman, and Timothy O'Leary. Learn more at www.unsolicitedpress.com.

CPSIA information can be obtained
at www.ICGtesting.com
Printed in the USA
LVHW061345090819
627122LV00003B/10/P